POP CULTURE BIOS
SUPER SINGERS

ONE
DIRECTION

BREAKOUT BOY BAND

MARCIA AMIDON LUSTED

Lerner Publications Company
MINNEAPOLIS

Lerner Publications Company
A division of Lerner Publishing Group, Inc.
241 First Avenue North
Minneapolis, MN 55401 U.S.A.

Website address: www.lernerbooks.com

Library of Congress Cataloging-in-Publication Data

Lusted, Marcia Amidon.
    One Direction : breakout boy band / by Marcia Amidon
Lusted.
        p.   cm. — (Pop culture bios. Super singers)
    Includes bibliographical references and index.
    ISBN 978-1-4677-0877-7 (lib. bdg. : alk. paper)
    1. One Direction (Musical group)—Juvenile literature.
2. Rock musicians—England—Biography—Juvenile literature.
I. Title.
ML3930.O66L87 2013
782.42164092'2—dc23 [B]   2012014921

Manufactured in the United States of America
1 – PP – 7/15/12

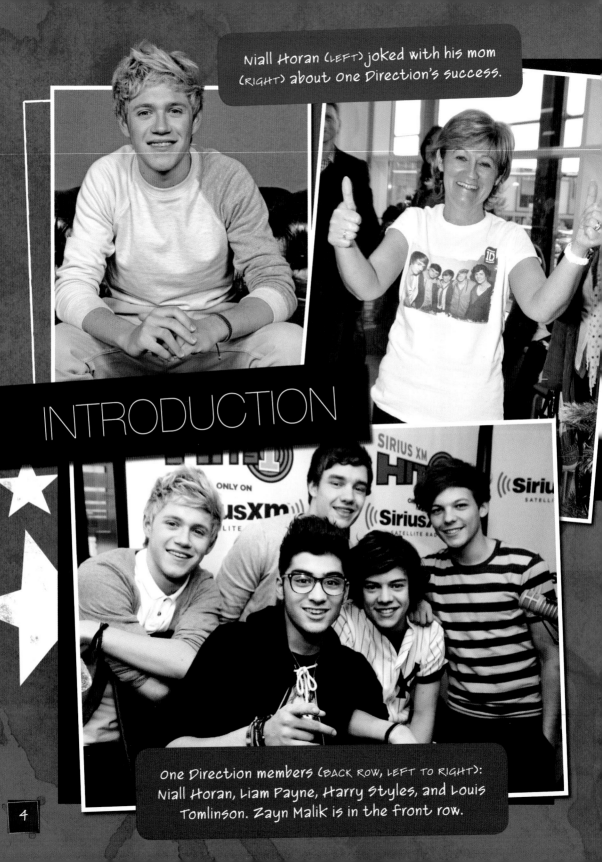

Niall Horan (LEFT) joked with his mom (RIGHT) about One Direction's success.

INTRODUCTION

One Direction members (BACK ROW, LEFT TO RIGHT): Niall Horan, Liam Payne, Harry Styles, and Louis Tomlinson. Zayn Malik is in the front row.

When One Direction's Niall Horan heard that the group's first album, *Up All Night*, had reached the top of *Billboard* magazine's U.S. album charts in just its first week, what did the Irish hottie do? "I freaked out!" he said. Then he tried to keep his mom from finding out so that he could play a trick on her. "I wanted to say that we had lost out," Niall laughed, "But *Billboard* had posted it on their website, so my cover was blown."

CHARTS =
lists of the best-selling music. If an album is on the top of the charts, it is selling well and is really popular!

One Direction member Harry Styles said about the epic news, "We're just five normal boys from the U.K. who've been given this opportunity, so we're having a great time working very hard."

'90S BABES ALL THE WAY

One Direction members Zayn Malik, Liam Payne, Harry Styles, and Louis Tomlinson were all born in the United Kingdom Niall Horan was born and raised in Ireland. Niall, Zayn, and Liam were born in 1993. Harry was born in 1994. Louis, the oldest One Direction member, was born in 1991.

It was just one more awesome thing for this adorbs five-member boy band. In just two years, they went from five talented strangers to a band going for the win on the British version of TV's *The X Factor*. How did this group (also known as 1D) become a fav with fans all over the world in such a short time? Read on to find out!

1D has quickly become a hit around the globe.

Niall Horan

Harry Styles

CHAPTER ONE

FIVE FEISTY GUYS

Zayn Malik

Louis Tomlinson

To get the real scoop on 1D, you have to go all the way back to the very beginning—when its members were just cute little kids! Some of the guys were musical even in early childhood. Niall remembers that the best Christmas present he ever got was a guitar. He used to sing in the car all the time too. "My aunt said she thought the radio was on [whenever I was with her]," Niall noted. Harry loved to sing as well and said that Elvis Presley was one of his favorite singers. Louis was actually an actor growing up. He appeared in a couple of British TV shows.

Liam was born with just one working kidney and nearly died at birth. He still has to be careful and be as healthy as possible. Liam admits that he was a bad boy at school—but at the same time, he was bullied by kids who were meaner and tougher than he was. He even ended up taking boxing lessons to defend himself from bullies. Since he loves to do anything active, he enjoyed the boxing lessons.

OUCH!

Liam remembers that his boxing lessons gave him confidence. But they also gave him a broken nose; a perforated eardrum; and a bruised, puffy face!

Liam Payne

Zayn spills that he was a handful when he was little. His mom would put him in his stroller even inside the house just to keep him out of trouble! He also remembers feeling as if he didn't fit in at school. He was the only mixed-heritage kid in his class. (His dad is from Pakistan, and his mom is British.)

Girl Crazy

The five guys definitely didn't start out as the heartthrobs they are now. None of them felt especially "cool" or popular with girls when they were growing up. But their time eventually came!

Zayn remembers moving to a new school where he finally fit in. All the girls wanted to know who the new kid was. "That's when I became cool," he recalled. He got his first kiss soon after that. He says that he was so short when he got the kiss that he had to stand on a brick to reach the girl's face!

Niall had his first kiss at eleven. The lucky lady was a foreign exchange student from France. Harry remembers having his first girlfriend at twelve. She was a girl named

HOT HAIR—OR NO HAIR

Zayn says that when he was twelve, he used to get up a half hour earlier than his sister just to do his hair! He admits he had some bad haircuts over the years. He even shaved his head a few times!

Emilie whom he is still friends with to this day.

Liam was well liked by classmates but couldn't get the attention of the girl he liked best. He asked her out twenty-two times, but she always said no. "Finally I sang to her, and she said she'd go out with me," Liam remembered. "But she dumped me the next day." These days, *tons* of girls wish Liam would sing to them the way he did to his crush!

Getting Their Start

The five future band buds had never met when they all auditioned for *The X Factor* back in 2010. They each tried out to be solo acts on the show. But none of them made the cut! Then one of the judges got the awesome idea to put the five guys together in a band. The judge thought they could compete in the group category. Everyone loved the idea—and that's how 1D was born!

1D stops for a quick pic before going into the studio to film an episode of *The X Factor* in 2010.

CHAPTER TWO

SHOWTIME

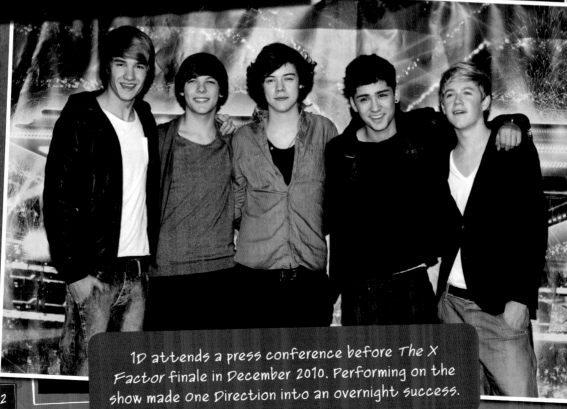

1D attends a press conference before *The X Factor* finale in December 2010. Performing on the show made One Direction into an overnight success.

So how did 1D get to be an *X Factor* success story? Well, at the beginning of the competition, they sailed through week after week. *X Factor* viewers *adored* the good-looking, talented guys. By week ten, in December 2010, most of the other acts had been eliminated. It was down to three competitors: solo singers Rebecca Ferguson and Matt Cardle and 1D. Many viewers were *sure* that 1D would win. Even judge Louis Walsh said, "I've never seen a band cause so much hysteria so early in their career!" But what happened next was a surprise.

Rebecca Ferguson and Matt Cardle competed against 1D on *The X Factor*.

LIAM MINI BIO

Likes: aftershave, surprises, singing in the shower

Dislikes: spoons (he used to "drink" his cereal and Jello out of a mug), flying

Favorite color: blue (he loves denim)

Most likely to: ask a girl out by singing

HARRY MINI BIO

Likes: Laser Quest laser tag, impressing girls with his curly hair
Dislikes: roller coasters, olives, swearing
Favorite color: pink
Most likely to: say exactly what he thinks on live TV

The End...but the Beginning

1D sang its song "Torn," which was also the first song the boys had ever sung together as a group.

NIALL MINI BIO

Likes: soccer, Spanish girls with nice smiles
Dislikes: clowns, going too long without food
Favorite color: yellow
Most likely to: Make Simon Cowell (from *The X Factor*) feel old by calling him "Uncle Si"

Then it was time to vote. When the final audience votes were added up, 1D came in last! Simon Cowell, a judge and the creator of *The X Factor*, seemed upset by the results. He spilled to the guys, "I am as proud of you as people as I am as artists."

It was clear that Cowell really liked 1D. And what happened after that is what turned the band into an international success.

LOUIS MINI BIO

Likes: sunbathing, Emma Watson (from the *Harry Potter* movies), silly voices
Dislikes: smoking, being pale
Favorite color: purple
Most likely to: play a practical joke

Likes: dancing, scary movies, new sneakers
Dislikes: open water (he can't swim),
sandwich crusts, pajamas
Favorite color: red
Most likely to: challenge you to a dance-off

Cowell offered the guys a recording contract. They were thrilled! They signed with Cowell's recording label, Syco Records. The band got more than $3 million in the deal—no kidding! 1D was on its way to a totally awesome career in pop.

Simon Cowell (HOLDING MICROPHONE) with Rebecca Ferguson (LEFT) and One Direction

CHAPTER THREE

MAKING IT BIG

Other losing acts on *The X Factor* just had to pack up and go home. But 1D went on the X Factor Live Tour in the United Kingdom for three months. At the same time, the boys made their first album, *Up All Night*. They released their first single, a song called "What Makes You Beautiful," in September of 2011. It got an amazing response from fans, hitting No. 1 on the British charts.

SINGLE =
a song that is released by itself instead of on an album along with other songs

The X Factor Live Tour was a huge hit with fans of One Direction.

Hitting the Road

Right after they hit the U.K. charts, the guys went on another U.K. tour. Tickets for shows sold out in just minutes! The tour was a complete success, and the band announced that it would be touring the United States in early 2012. The band also picked up the Brit Award for Best British Single for "What Makes You Beautiful." Harry Styles told the audience, "We want to say, again, a massive thank you to the fans. Everything we do is for you, so this is yours. Thank you so much."

Winning a Brit Award was a big deal for the boys.

THE BEATLES, TAKE 2

Some people like to compare 1D to the 1960s musical group The Beatles (LEFT). They also came from the United Kingdom and became famous all over the world (and still are!). Fans became hysterical every time The Beatles showed up.

One Direction hit U.S. shores in March. Their album had become the first ever debut album by a British band to start at No. 1 on the U.S. music charts. One of the first things the guys did in the United States was to sing on the *Today* show in New York. The scene outside the studio was crazy! Fans gathered in a giant screaming mass, waving signs and clutching cell phones poised to snap pics of the band.

The guys signed copies of *Up All Night* for tons of fans in New York.

One Direction on *Today*

"Pretty Amazing"

Many more TV appearances came after *Today*. In March 2012, the guys appeared on the Nickelodeon Kids' Choice Awards. As 1D came onstage, fans cheered and even burst into tears at the sight of the band. The boys broke into their hit song "What Makes You Beautiful." Everyone in the audience clapped and sang along— even Selena Gomez, Taylor Swift, and First Lady Michelle Obama!

WHAT ARE THE FIVE GUYS' FAVORITE FOODS TO COOK?

Niall: spaghetti Bolognese

Liam: fajitas

Louis: cereal (you guessed it...cooking isn't Louis's thing!)

Harry: beef Wellington

Zayn: fried chicken

LOOK OUT FOR THE...PIGEON? O_o

Niall's biggest fear isn't spiders, heights, or the dark. It's pigeons! He's been afraid of them since he was a kid. The band's security guards have to chase away any pigeons that get too close to him.

In April 2012, 1D was invited to be the musical guests on *Saturday Night Live*. Niall told MTV, "We obviously get American TV in the U.K., and I've watched *Saturday Night Live* before and [it's] a big, big deal; everyone knows that. And when we got invited on, we couldn't believe it.... We haven't spent a lot of time here, so a lot of people don't know who we are, so to be invited on such a prestigious American show is pretty amazing."

One Direction was thrilled to perform on Saturday Night Live.

CHAPTER FOUR

IT'S NOT EASY BEING FAMOUS

Fans in Los Angeles were pumped to see 1D.

The five guys in One Direction are fan favs because they're just so darling. But they're still not used to all the attention they get from girls. One girl flew all the way from Australia to the United States on her birthday just to meet the band at an airport!

One Direction will keep on touring and performing. But what's it really like to be on the road, away from home for months? "We miss our families; we miss our friends. We get homesick, massively so," Niall confesses.

The guys have their tour manager, Paul, and a recording label executive, Lisa, to keep them in line when they travel. But 1D doesn't usually get too wild. They spend a lot of time on Facebook, Twitter, and their phones, texting and messaging their friends and fans.

Tour manager Paul (STANDING) keeps a watchful eye on excited fans.

Touring is exhausting, though, and sometimes they need to let loose. There have been some epic moments when Paul had to play the dad. The guys had a food fight in a New Jersey shopping center once. They ended up throwing paper plates around. At a bowling alley in New York, they tried throwing three balls down the lane at once, just for fun, and broke some equipment. "A guy fixed it in twenty minutes with a screwdriver," one of the guys remembered. "We were just having a laugh." They've also been known to sneak out for a little basic fun, like a late-night game of soccer in Boston Garden.

FAIL!

At the 2012 Brit Awards, Harry accidentally thanked the wrong radio station (oops!) in his acceptance speech. The band later sent out an apology, but not before its songs were temporarily banned from the ignored radio station (Capital FM).

A Few Squabbles

Touring can also mean a little *too* much "together time" for the guys. Spending lots of time in close quarters can make the bandmates sort of stabby. They sometimes argue with one another. But in the end, they're still best friends. "We don't have big fights, more like brotherly squabbles," Harry explains. Liam adds, "At the end of the day, it's about getting to travel the world with your best mates."

The group also knows that a lot of people think they're just another boy band. Sometimes they don't feel as if they're taken seriously. Niall told a Canadian newspaper, "People think that a boy band is [being] dressed in all one color. We're boys in a band. We're trying to do something different from what people would think is the typical kind of boy band. We're trying to do different kinds of music, and we're just trying to be ourselves."

A HUMBLE BAND

The 1D guys don't have big heads. Zayn sums up how they feel about themselves this way: "We're five normal lads, we're not massively ripped, we don't have amazing bodies, and we freely admit we can't dance." Now that's humility!

Getting Cozy

The guys also have had to get used to seeing their love lives in the news. Harry Styles went through a messy breakup with his GF, Caroline Flack. She was fourteen years older than him. These days Harry says that he's through with older women. Zayn once dated singer Rebecca Ferguson, whom he met on *The X Factor*.

The guys all admit that it's hard to be tight with a girlfriend when they're on the road. Liam has been seeing Danielle Peazer. But he kept his GF under wraps until they got publicly cozy at his eighteenth birthday party. Louis has recently dated Eleanor Calder, a model. Liam explains, "We can only have visitors between 7 and 8 pm because we're so busy during the day." That can make seeing their girlfriends pretty tricky!

GIRLS <3 HIM

According to the band, who's the most popular with girls? Harry!

Looking Ahead

One Direction has a lot going on. Their song "What Makes You Beautiful" was featured

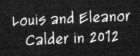

Louis and Eleanor Calder in 2012

on *Glee*. A book about the band called *Dare to Dream: Life as One Direction (below)* came out in May of 2012. It tells the story of the band and its members in the guys' own words. There's even a documentary called *One Direction: A Year in the Making* about the band's creation and how they became fan favs so quickly.

DOCUMENTARY =
a movie that tells the facts

The guys are eager to make a new album every year and to try some new and different sounds. That might include heavier drums and guitars and more of a live feel to their music. As Harry says, "It's important that we like what we're doing. It wouldn't be good if we weren't enjoying what we're doing… [but] we are!"

100% OFFICIAL

1D

With lots of exclusive photos! One Direction xx

DARE TO DREAM LIFE AS **ONE DIRECTION**

ONE DIRECTION PICS!

Louis

Liam

Zayn

SOURCE NOTES

5   Alicia Rancilio, "Up Is Only Direction for New Boy Band," *Chicago Sun Times*, March 24, 2012, http://www.suntimes.com/entertainment/music/11456746-421/up-is-only-direction-for-new-boy-band.html (April 16, 2012).

6   Ibid.

9   *Sun* (London), "Until 6th Form I Was So Short I Stood on a Brick to Kiss," September 17, 2011, http://www.thesun.co.uk/sol/homepage/showbiz/bizarre/3819612/Until-6th-form-I-was-so-short-I-stood-on-a-brickbr-to-kiss.html (April 16, 2012).

10   Ibid.

11   Ibid.

13   *Fanpop!,* "One Direction's Story…" n.d. http://www.fanpop.com/spots/one-direction/articles/82424/title/one-directions-story (April 16, 2012).

14   Ibid.

18   Carla Hay, "One Direction Issues Apology After Capital FM Backlash about Brit Awards Speech," *Examiner.com*, February 22, 2012, http://cdn2-b.examiner.com/the-x-factor-in-national/one-direction-issues-apology-after-capital-fm-backlash-about-brit-awards-speech (April 16, 2012).

21   Katie Byrne, "One Direction Get Celebs Dancing at Kids' Choice Awards," *MTV News*, March 31, 2012, http://www.mtv.com/news/articles/1682190/one-direction-kids-choice-awards-performance-2012.jhtml (April 16, 2012).

23   *STV* TV, "One Direction Lads Run Down and Massively Homesick," March, http://entertainment.stv.tv/music/301138-one-direction-lads-run-down-and-massively-homesick/ (April 16, 2012).

24   Matthew Wells, "'Hanging Out' with One Direction in the US," *BBC News*, March 22, 2012, http://www.bbc.co.uk/news/magazine-17465101?print=true (April 16, 2012).

25   Ibid.

25   Leah Collins, "One Direction is more than just another boy band," *National Post* (Toronto), March 12, 2012, http://arts.nationalpost.com/2012/03/12/one-direction-is-more-than-just-another-boy-band/ (April 16, 2012).

25   Will Payne, "We're Just Five Normal Lads Who Can't Dance and Don't Have Six-Packs," *Mirror* (London), September 11, 2011, http://www.mirror.co.uk/3am/celebrity-news/one-direction--were-just-152968 (April 16, 2012).

26   *STV* TV, "One Direction Open Up about Girlfriends, Little Mix and Amelia Lily," February 2, 2012, http://entertainment.stv.tv/showbiz/296025-one-direction-open-up-about-girlfriends-little-mix-and-amelia-lily/ (April 16, 2012).

27   Collins, "One Direction."

MORE ONE DIRECTION INFO

Oliver, Sarah. *One Direction A–Z*. London: John Blake Publishing, 2011. Read twenty-six fascinating facts about the band and their rise to fame!

One Direction
http://www.onedirectionmusic.com/gb/home
Check out the band's official website, where you'll find news, upcoming events, videos, music, and more.

One Direction. *One Direction: Dare to Dream: Life as One Direction*. New York: HarperCollins, 2012. Learn more about 1D in their own words.

One Direction. *1D One Direction: Forever Young*. London: HarperCollins UK, 2012. This British book about the band is also written in 1D's own words.

Parker, Evie. *100% One Direction: The 100% Unofficial Biography*. London: Transworld Publishers, 2011. Parker tells everything you need to know about the five adorable guys of 1D.

Roberts, Jeremy. *The Beatles: Music Revolutionaries*. Minneapolis: Twenty-First Century Books, 2011.

INDEX

The images in this book are used with the permission of: © Mathis Wienand/Getty Images, pp. 2, 22 (top); © Jo Hale/Getty Images, pp. 3 (top), 29 (bottom); © Michael Kovac/WireImage/Getty Images, pp. 3 (bottom), 28 (bottom); IBL/Rex USA, pp. 4 (top left), 28 (top right); JD1 WENN Photos/Newscom, p. 4 (top right); © Astrid Stawiarz/Getty Images, p. 4 (bottom); © Michael Loccisano/Getty Images, p. 5; Newspix/Rex USA, pp. 6, 7; © Scott Legato/Getty Images, p. 8 (top left); © Gareth Cattermole/Getty Images, p. 8 (top right); © Mike Marsland/WireImage/Getty Images, p. 8 (bottom left and bottom right); LTA WENN Photos/Newscom, p. 9; © Danny Martindale/FilmMagic/Getty Images, p. 11; Press Association via AP Images, p. 12 (top); © Dave Hogan/Getty Images, pp. 12 (bottom), 13; Ken McKay/Rex USA, p. 15; © Martin Harris/Capital Pictures/Retna Ltd., p. 16 (top); JRAA/ZDS WENN Photos/Newscom, p. 16 (bottom); © Duncan Bryceland/UPPA/ZUMA Press, p. 17; David Fisher/Rex USA, p. 18; © David Farrell/Redferns/Getty Images, p. 19 (top); © Janette Pellegrini/WireImage/Getty Images, p. 19 (bottom); © Al Pereira/WireImage/Getty Images, p. 20; © Dana Edelson/NBC/NBCU Photo Bank via Getty Images, p. 21; © Splash News/CORBIS, pp. 22 (bottom), 24, 26; © Adam Bettcher/Getty Images, p. 23; AP Photo/HarperCollins Children's Books, p. 27; © Ilya S. Savenok/Getty Images, p. 28 (top left); © George Pimentel/WireImage/Getty Images, p. 29 (top left); Matt Baron/BEImages/Rex USA, p. 29 (top center); © Dave M. Benett/Getty Images, p. 29 (right).

Front cover: © Venturelli/Getty Images (left); © Jon Furniss/WireImage/Getty Images (right).
Back cover: © Jo Hale/Getty Images.

Main body text set in Shannon Std Book 12/18.
Typeface provided by Monotype Typography.